Today's Superstars
Entertainment

Johnny Depp

by William David Thomas

GARETH STEVENS
GS
PUBLISHING
A Member of the WRC Media Family of Companies

Please visit our web site at: www.garethstevens.com
For a free color catalog describing Gareth Stevens Publishing's
list of high-quality books and multimedia programs, call
1-800-542-2595 (USA) or 1-800-387-3178 (Canada).
Gareth Stevens Publishing's fax: (414) 332-3567.

Library of Congress Cataloging-in-Publication Data

Thomas, William David.
   Johnny Depp / by William David Thomas.
      p. cm. — (Today's superstars. Entertainment)
   Includes bibliographical references and index.
   ISBN-13: 978-0-8368-7650-5 (lib. bdg.)
   1. Depp, Johnny—Juvenile literature. 2. Motion picture actors
and actresses—United States—Biography—Juvenile literature. I. Title.
PN2287.D39A32   2006
791.4302'8'092—dc22   2006030683

This edition first published in 2007 by
Gareth Stevens Publishing
A Member of the WRC Media Family of Companies
330 West Olive Street, Suite 100
Milwaukee, WI 53212 USA

Editor: Gini Holland
Art direction and design: Tammy West
Picture research: Sabrina Crewe

Photo credits: cover © Walt Disney/courtesy•Everett Collection; p. 5 Everett
Collection; p. 7 © Peter Mountain/Industrial Light & Magic/Bureau L.A.
Collection/Corbis; p. 9 Time Life Pictures/ Getty Images; p. 11 © Deborah
Feingold/Corbis; p. 14 New Line Cinema/Everett Collection; p. 16 Orion Picture
Corp./Everett Collection; p. 17 © Stephen J. Cannell Productions/courtesy
Everett Collection; p. 19 © 20th Century Fox/courtesy Everett Collection; p. 20
© Murray Andrew/Corbis Sygma; p. 22 Getty Images; p. 25 © Miramax/courtesy
Everett Collection; p. 27 © Fred Prouser/Reuters/Corbis; p. 28 © Warner
Brothers/courtesy Everett Collection

Printed in the United States of America

1 2 3 4 5 6 7 8 9 10 10 09 08 07

Contents

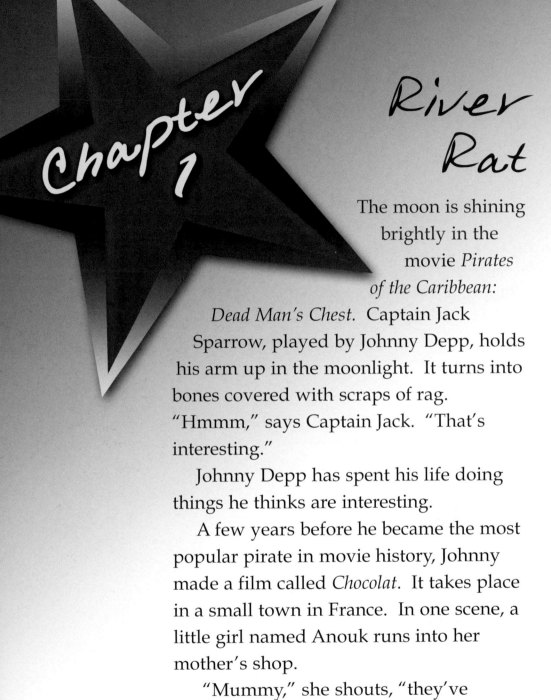

Chapter 1

River Rat

The moon is shining
brightly in the
movie *Pirates
of the Caribbean:
Dead Man's Chest.* Captain Jack
Sparrow, played by Johnny Depp, holds
his arm up in the moonlight. It turns into
bones covered with scraps of rag.
"Hmmm," says Captain Jack. "That's
interesting."

Johnny Depp has spent his life doing
things he thinks are interesting.

A few years before he became the most
popular pirate in movie history, Johnny
made a film called *Chocolat.* It takes place
in a small town in France. In one scene, a
little girl named Anouk runs into her
mother's shop.

"Mummy," she shouts, "they've
landed!"

"Who?"

"Pirates!"

They hurry down to the river. Instead of pirate ships, they find some houseboats tied up by the shore. The people on the boats travel from town to town. They play music and do odd jobs for money. The town folks don't trust them and call them "river rats."

Anouk and her mom find their raggedy leader. He is sitting on his boat, playing a guitar. Anouk asks him, "What's a river rat? Is it like a pirate?"

"Yeah, I guess you could say that," replies Johnny Depp.

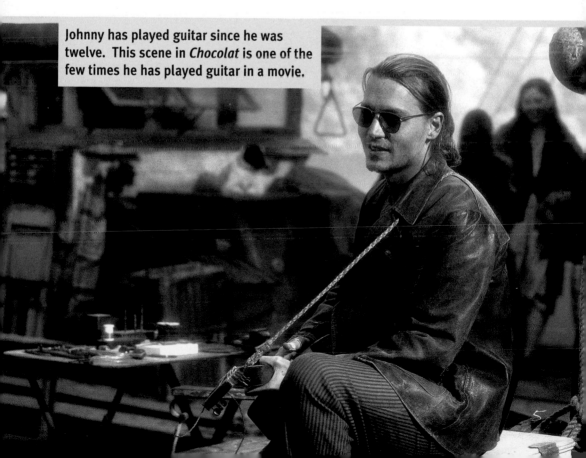

Johnny has played guitar since he was twelve. This scene in *Chocolat* is one of the few times he has played guitar in a movie.

5

Johnny's character is named Roux (pronounced ROO). Later in the movie he rescues Anouk's mother when the boats burn. Roux also helps Anouk with her imaginary pet, a kangaroo.

In many ways, the "river rat" in that film is a lot like the real Johnny Depp. He has spent a lot of time moving from place to place. He usually does what he wants, instead of what others expect him to do. That makes some people nervous, so they don't always trust him. Johnny likes to wear raggedy clothes and play his guitar. He is loyal to his friends. He is kind and loving toward children. Like the river rat, he has found happiness living in France.

Johnny Depp was a troubled — and trouble-making — teenager who dreamed of being a rock star. Now he is one of the biggest stars in Hollywood. Johnny once said, "I know it sounds strange, but . . . I never really wanted to be an actor. . . . I was a musician, and still am. The other stuff just happened." How that other stuff happened is quite a story.

Fact File

Johnny often wears ski caps or old-style hats. An interviewer once asked him why he liked funny hats. He replied, "I don't know. Maybe I just read too much Dr. Seuss as a kid."

Being Different

Johnny has played many different kinds of characters in his movies. Some of them have been really strange. Johnny was once asked if people could learn anything from those characters. He said, "I hope it would be that it's okay to be different from the crowd. . . . We should really question ourselves before we pass judgment on someone who is different from us."

In *Pirates of the Caribbean: Dead Man's Chest*, Johnny was the guest of some cannibals. He decided not to stay for dinner.

Chapter 2

Guitar Dreams

It's fun to imagine that Johnny Depp was born at sea on a pirate ship. Actually, John Christopher Depp II was born in Owensboro, Kentucky, on June 9, 1963. His dad, John, was an engineer for the city. His mother, Betty Sue, was a waitress in a local café. Johnny was the fourth, and youngest, child in the family. He has a brother, Danny, and two sisters — Debbie and Christie.

When Johnny was six, the family left Kentucky. They moved to Miramar, Florida, near Miami. For almost a year, they lived in a small hotel while Johnny's father looked for work. Over the next few years, the family moved more than thirty times. They lived in houses, apartments, and motels.

Johnny was always "the new kid" in school. He was shy, and he had a hard time making friends. He spent a lot of time alone, watching television and listening to music. Johnny became a big fan of old horror movies, such as Frankenstein and Dracula. His favorite band was the rock group Kiss.

When he was twelve, Johnny bought an electric guitar for $25. He spent hours each day teaching himself how to play. He dreamed of becoming a rock star.

In 1995, Johnny was in Los Angeles for the first showing of his film, *Nick of Time*. His special guest was his mother, Betty Sue. Johnny has remained very close to his mom.

Divorce and Marriage

Johnny's parents were not happy. Moving to Florida had been hard for them. By the mid-1970s, their marriage was falling apart. They fought often, and Johnny began staying away from home. When Johnny was fifteen, his parents divorced. His father moved out of the house, and Johnny has rarely seen him since.

Soon after the divorce, his mom got sick. Johnny said it was because her heart was broken. His brother and sisters had left home by then, and Johnny cared for his mom by himself.

He put lots of time and energy into music. Johnny formed a band with a few friends. At first, they played at backyard parties. In the early 1980s, they began playing at local music clubs. Because all of the band members were under eighteen, the club owners had to sneak them in the back door.

Music was all Johnny cared about. He had little

Fact File

When he was about fourteen, Johnny tried to get away from his parents' fighting. He moved out of the house. For a few months, he lived in the back of a car owned by one of his buddies, Sal Jenco.

Daredevil Dreams

One of Johnny's childhood heroes was Evel Knievel. Evel
was a daredevil. He rode his motorcycle through walls
of fire and jumped it over rows of cars. Johnny dreamed
of performing his own wild stunts. He sometimes called
himself "Awful Knawful."

Johnny's first love was music,
not acting. He has played
guitar with live bands and
on several recordings.

time for — or interest in — school. He skipped most of his classes. After two years in high school, he quit for good. He worked in gas stations during the day and played in bands at night.

One of Johnny's bands was called The Kids. A member of the band introduced Johnny to his sister. She was a musician too, and they began dating. Within a few months, Lori Ann Allison and Johnny were married. Lori joined the band.

The Kids were good enough to be the opening act for some big name bands and recording artists. One of them was Iggy Pop, a star Johnny had loved as a boy. The Kids began to dream of making it big in the music world. They thought they could get more work — and more attention — in Los Angeles. They hoped that maybe, just maybe, they could get a recording deal.

Fact File

Johnny's first band was called The Flame. To look like a rock star, he wore his mother's velvet shirts on stage. He also wore bell-bottomed pants and platform shoes.

Jump!

Chapter 3

In 1984, Johnny and The Kids packed their stuff and drove to California. They changed the band's name to Six Gun Method. It sounded more powerful. Their big dreams, however, soon became nightmares. The music business in Los Angeles was a lot tougher than it was in Florida. "There were so many bands," Johnny said, "it was impossible to make any money."

At the same time, his marriage to Lori was failing. Johnny remembered his parents' divorce and tried to make the marriage work. He realized, however, that he and Lori were no longer right for each other. They divorced in 1985.

Just when it seemed that nothing was going right, Johnny met a young actor named Nicolas Cage. He helped Johnny try out for a part in a movie. The film was called *A Nightmare on Elm Street*. Johnny got the job. His character spoke only a few lines and was soon killed by a monster named Freddy Krueger. The part was small, but it was the beginning of something new.

Johnny got small parts in a few more films and television shows. He didn't earn much money and had trouble paying his rent. He wondered if his acting career, like his music career, might fail.

Then Johnny got a small role in a movie about the Vietnam War. It was called *Platoon*. The film won the Academy

Johnny played a teenager named Glen Lantz in " his first movie, *A Nightmare on Elm Street*. Johnny says that when he was actually a teenager in Florida, " None of the girls wanted to hang out with me. I was just, you know, a weird kid."

Award for Best Picture in 1986. It was an important movie. Because Johnny was part of it, more people in Hollywood began to think of him as a serious actor.

Becoming a Star

One of those people was a television producer. He was planning a new series. It was about undercover police officers who worked in high schools. Johnny really didn't want to work on the show. He hoped to make more movies. He needed money, however, so he finally accepted the job. He had to sign a six-year contract.

The show was called *21 Jump Street*. It became a big success. Johnny's personality and good looks attracted lots of viewers. He began getting thousands of fan letters. His picture was used to advertise the show. The program made him a star.

Family and Friends

21 Jump Street was filmed in Vancouver, Canada. It took nine months to make the first year's programs. Johnny asked his

Fact File

Johnny's movie career was the end of his band. He had to leave for six weeks to make *Nightmare on Elm Street*. The other band members gave up.

Johnny (*above, far right*) learned to speak some Vietnamese for his part in the 1986 film, *Platoon*. The film's director, Oliver Stone, had been a soldier in the Vietnam War.

mother to come to Vancouver to keep him company. One of his childhood friends, Sal Jenco, also came for a visit. Sal hung around with Johnny so much that he finally got a small part in the series.

Johnny didn't want play the same character all of the time. He wanted to do other roles as well. After two years, he tried to get out of his contract. The producers wouldn't let him. They knew he was the main reason people watched the program every week. Johnny began to argue with the show's producers and writers. He had disagreements with the other actors. No one on the show was happy — especially Johnny.

On A Lunch Box

Being a star was hard for Johnny. He lost all of his privacy. He said, "Suddenly, you go into a restaurant and people are pointing at you and whispering." He felt he was no longer himself. He was just a celebrity. "They turned me into a product," he said, "and I didn't have a say in it." Actress Holly Peete co-starred with Johnny on *21 Jump Street*. She said, "He just hated the idea of being on a lunch box or some teenage girl's wall."

In the TV series *21 Jump Street*, Johnny (*center*) played an undercover cop pretending to be a high school student.

Fact File

To pay his bills, Johnny once sold pens over the telephone. Sometimes he used made-up names and strange voices. He called it "my first job as an actor."

17

Chapter 4

Runs With Scissors

Things got better for Johnny in 1989. After nearly three years, he was released from his *21 Jump Street* contract. Soon after that, he met a young actress named Winona Ryder. They hit it off right away and began dating. Then he was chosen to star with Winona in a new movie. It would be the movie that made him famous.

The film was called *Edward Scissorhands*. It's about a young man who is created by a scientist. The scientist dies before the man is finished. Edward grows up with scissors where his hands should be. People are afraid of him and make fun of him. Johnny really liked the character. He said, "There's quite a lot of Edward in me, and a lot of me in him." The movie

The Little Tramp

Charlie Chaplin was a superstar in the early days of Hollywood. Back then, all movies were silent. The films did not have voices, sounds, or music. Actors had to tell their stories by using their eyes and body movements. Charlie Chaplin, known as "the little tramp," was a master at this. Johnny's character in *Edward Scissorhands* rarely speaks. To make people understand what Edward was thinking and feeling, Johnny studied Charlie Chaplin's silent films. He copied many of Chaplin's actions, especially his famous walk.

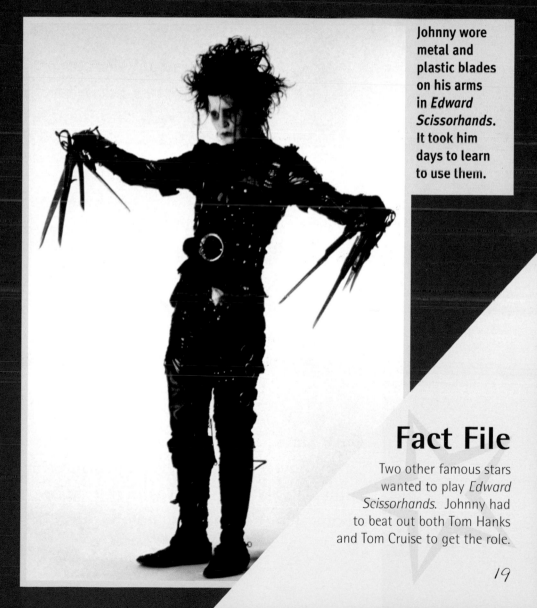

Johnny wore metal and plastic blades on his arms in *Edward Scissorhands*. It took him days to learn to use them.

Fact File

Two other famous stars wanted to play *Edward Scissorhands*. Johnny had to beat out both Tom Hanks and Tom Cruise to get the role.

19

was a hit. Suddenly, Johnny Depp was the talk of Hollywood.

As an established star, Johnny could choose the films and the roles he wanted. The ones he picked to do were not always successful. But Johnny looked for stories and characters that interested him. He said, "I do what I want and, if it works within my career, great. If not . . . I won't be a slave to success."

Although he was now a full-time actor, Johnny still loved music. In 1993, he bought a nightclub in Hollywood called the Viper Room. It became quite popular. Famous musicians like Johnny Cash, Bruce Springsteen, and Sheryl Crow played there. Once in a while, so did Johnny.

Dark Days

On Halloween night, 1993, a young actor named River Phoenix was in the Viper Room. He collapsed outside the club.

Johnny's life off-screen was falling apart in 1994. When he was acting, however, he was very professional. He was also very kind. People who worked with him praised him. Sarah Jessica Parker worked with him in the film *Ed Wood*. She said, "He's the star, but he's always running around asking if you need water or anything." His co-star in *What's Eating Gilbert Grape?* was Leonardo DiCaprio. Leo said, "There's an element of Johnny that's extremely nice, and extremely cool . . . ."

Later that night, Phoenix died from a drug overdose.

Some newspapers and magazines blamed Johnny. They said he allowed drugs to be sold and used at the club. Johnny said that wasn't true, but not everyone believed him. At about the same time, Johnny was breaking up with Winona Ryder. In January, 1994, his Los Angeles home was destroyed by an earthquake.

These events hurt Johnny badly. He felt angry. His behavior became wild and reckless. He used drugs, drank a lot, and slept very little. One night, he was rushed to a hospital and nearly died. He finally got frightened enough to change his ways. He came out of these dark days by concentrating on his acting.

Fact File

Johnny has always liked to dress in ragged jeans and T-shirts. In 1993, *People* magazine named him one of the worst dressed celebrities. Johnny said, "I'm proud. My goal is to be the number one worst dressed."

Two Rebels

One person who helped Johnny come out of his dark days was the great actor Marlon Brando. They made a film together called *Don Juan DeMarco.* Brando understood what Johnny was going through. As a young actor, he too had been a rebel and a wild troublemaker. Johnny said, "He saw me going through stuff he had been through." Brando had changed. Johnny knew he could, too.

Marlon Brando (*left*) starred with Johnny in the movie *Don Juan de Marco.* Movie critics consider Brando one of the greatest American actors of all time. Johnny said it was an honor to work with him.

Pretty Cool

Johnny's acting earned him a lot of praise. Movie critics loved his work in *Donnie Brasco*. That was the true story of an undercover FBI agent. *Sleepy Hollow* was the retelling of an old ghost story. At the time, it was Johnny's biggest money-maker. *Chocolat* was the film where he played the "river rat." It was nominated for five Academy Awards.

Johnny's personal life was not going as well as his acting. Like many Hollywood stars, he found it hard to date people. Every time he went out with a girl, they were followed by photographers and newspaper writers. When he broke up with Winona Ryder, Johnny said it was because the media would not leave them alone.

Parenthood, Pirates, and Peter Pan

In 1998, he met a French singer-actress named Vanessa Paradis. They've been together ever since. Johnny bought a large home in the French countryside. It's far away from photographers and writers. He and Vanessa now live there for much of each year.

Their first child, a girl named Lily-Rose Melody, was born in 1999. Becoming a father changed Johnny. He said, "This baby has given me life. When my daughter was born . . . I wasn't angry any more." Johnny quit his reckless ways. He did diaper duty and took Lily-Rose for walks in her stroller. Their second child, Jack, was born in 2002.

Johnny loves the quiet life in France, away from the hustle and attention of Hollywood. He says, "I'll take the kids and we'll go out on the swing set . . . and we'll stop by the garden and see how the tomatoes are doing."

Johnny watched a lot of Disney movies with his kids. He thought it would be fun to be in a film like that. He asked the Disney studios if he could be the voice

Fact File

Johnny sometimes gets famous musicians to play at his nightclub. Their music raises money for the Starlight Children's Foundation. This group helps children with cancer and other serious conditions.

Becoming an Actor

When Johnny started acting, he took classes. Later he studied with a famous acting coach. He also read lots of books on acting. One book said that actors should not play a character, they should become that character. Johnny has become famous for taking on the personality of his characters.

of a character in a cartoon film. The studio had a better idea. They wanted him to be a pirate.

Johnny took the role of Captain Jack Sparrow in *Pirates of the Caribbean: The Curse of the Black Pearl*. When he first read the script he said, "I felt nine years old again." The movie was a huge success. Johnny was nominated for an Academy Award as Best Actor.

The next year, he was nominated for the Best Actor award again. This time, it was for his work in *Finding Neverland*. He played James Barrie, the man who wrote the stage play and story called *Peter Pan*.

Then, in the summer of 2006, Johnny went back to sea. *Pirates of the Caribbean: Dead Man's Chest* was a box office hit the day it opened. It sold $132 million worth of tickets in its first three days. No other movie had ever done that.

Where will Johnny Depp go next? He'll be back as Captain Jack in the next *Pirates of the Caribbean* film. He might return to his old

Fact File

Vanessa often brought Lily-Rose to visit Johnny when he was filming *Pirates of the Caribbean*. Later they had a shock. Lily-Rose thought her dad really was a pirate!

Wish Upon a Star

Johnny tries to give back as much as possible in return for his great success. One of the projects he supports is the Make-a-Wish Foundation. This group raises money to grant the wishes of children who are very sick. Many of them are dying. Johnny visits these children in hospitals. When possible, he takes them to visit movie sets. He says, "The most courageous people I've met have been nine years old."

Vanessa Paradis came to Los Angeles with Johnny in 2005. In a special ceremony, his footprints and hand prints were added to a sidewalk there.

Johnny (*above, in the black hat*) played candy bar maker Willie Wonka in *Charlie and the Chocolate Factory*. A few years earlier, he appeared in *Chocolat*. While he was making that movie, he ate so much chocolate that he grew to hate it.

television show. Some people in Hollywood have been talking about making a movie about *21 Jump Street*.

Johnny once said, "Maybe one day I'll make a movie that really blows people away. The sort of movie I can point to one night when I'm a real old man watching TV and say to my grandchildren, 'Hey guys, Grandpop was pretty cool in this film, don't you think?'"

Odds are, they will think Johnny Depp was pretty cool.

Time Line

1963 John Christopher Depp II is born on June 9, in Owensboro, Kentucky.

1983 Moves to Los Angeles with his rock band, The Kids.

1984 First movie role in *Nightmare on Elm Street*.

1987 Television series *21 Jump Street* begins.

1990 Becomes a star as *Edward Scissorhands*.

1998 Meets French actress-singer Vanessa Paradis

1999 Daughter, Lily-Rose Melody Depp, is born.

2002 Son, John Christopher Depp III ("Jack") is born.

2003 Nominated for the Best Actor Academy Award for *Pirates of the Caribbean: The Curse of the Black Pearl*.

2004 *Finding Neverland* brings another Best Actor Academy Award nomination.

2006 *Pirates of the Caribbean: Dead Man's Chest* is a huge box office hit.

Glossary

Academy Award – the top award given by the American movie industry. It is also called an Oscar.

celebrity – someone famous.

contract – a written and signed agreement to do something.

director – the person who supervises the making of a movie.

media – newspapers, magazines, radio, and television.

movie critics – people who make their living by giving opinions about movies.

nominated – named to be voted on for an award.

personality – someone's behavior, values, looks, and speech.

producer – someone who raises money and hires people to make a movie or television show.

scene – a small part of a movie, play, or television show.

To Find Out More

Books

Johnny Depp. People in the News (series). Kara Higgins
   (Lucent Books)

Johnny Depp. Superstars of Film (series). Esme Hawes
   (Chelsea House Publishers)

Videos

Charlie and the Chocolate Factory (Warner Brothers) PG

Chocolat (Miramax) PG-13

Cry-Baby (Imagine Entertainment) PG-13

Pirates of the Caribbean: The Curse of the Black Pearl
   (Walt Disney Studios) PG-13

What's Eating Gilbert Grape (Paramount Studios) PG-13

Web Sites

Johnny Depp.Com
www.johnnydepp.com
Information about Johnny's life and movies

The Johnny Depp Zone
www.johnnydepp-zone.com
Interviews with Johnny, plus film and voice clips

Publishers note to educators and parents: Our editors have carefully
reviewed these Web sites to ensure that they are suitable for children.
Many Web sites change frequently, however, and we cannot guarantee
that a site's future contents will continue to meet our high standards
of quality and educational value. Be advised that children should be
closely supervised whenever they access the Internet.

Index

About the Author

William David Thomas lives in Rochester, New York, where he works with students who have special needs. He has written software documentation, magazine articles, training programs, annual reports, books for children, one song, a few poems, and lots of letters. Bill claims he was once King of Fiji, but gave up the throne to pursue a career as a relief pitcher. It's not true.